Various Lies

poems by

Elizabeth McMunn-Tetangco

Finishing Line Press
Georgetown, Kentucky

Various Lies

Copyright © 2016 by Elizabeth McMunn-Tetangco
ISBN 978-1-63534-036-5 First Edition
All rights reserved under International and Pan-American Copyright Conventions.
No part of this book may be reproduced in any manner whatsoever without written permission from the publisher, except in the case of brief quotations embodied in critical articles and reviews.

ACKNOWLEDGMENTS

VARIOUS DISTANCES (first appeared in *Hobart*)
YELLOW HOUSE (first appeared in *The Lake*)
VELELLA (first appeared in *The Más Tequila Review*)
BATS (first appeared in *The Kentucky Review*)
COYOTES (first appeared in *The Kentucky Review*)
DOCKS (first appeared in *Word Riot*)
LUCKY (first appeared in *The Lake*)
BEFORE I LOST YOU (first appeared in *Hobart*)
THE FIRST BIRD (first appeared in *The Merced River Literary Review*)
PARACHUTES (first appeared in *Paper Nautilus*)
PETRICHOR (first appeared in *The Camel Saloon*)
THEFT (first appeared in *Paper Nautilus*)
STICKERS (first appeared in *Paper Nautilus*)
SKATER (first appeared in *The Potomac Review*)
MORNING SKY (first appeared in *The Curator*)
PAPER DOLL (first appeared in *The Lake*)

Warm thanks to the journals in which some of these poems previously appeared, namely, *Hobart*; *The Lake*; *The Más Tequila Review*; *The Kentucky Review*; *Word Riot*; *The Merced River Literary Review*; *Paper Nautilus*; *The Camel Saloon*; *The Potomac Review*; *The Curator*. Additional thanks are due to Meg Withers, a generous and talented wordsmith who has graciously supported, encouraged, and appreciated my work and who has inspired and nurtured so many new—and not-so-new—poets. I would be remiss if I did not also thank Anne, Dawn, Bonnie, Stacie, and Shane for their feedback and friendship, and my parents for their unwavering support of my crazy dreams. Lastly, thank you to Keith and James—I love you.

Publisher: Leah Maines
Editor: Christen Kincaid
Cover Art: Elizabeth McMunn-Tetangco
Author Photo: Keith Tetangco
Cover Design: Elizabeth Maines

Printed in the USA on acid-free paper.
Order online: www.finishinglinepress.com
          also available on amazon.com

Author inquiries and mail orders:
Finishing Line Press
P. O. Box 1626
Georgetown, Kentucky 40324
U. S. A.

Table of Contents

Various Distances 1

Setting Fires 2

Loose 4

The Baby 5

Yellow House 6

Velella 7

Bats 9

Coyotes 11

Docks 13

Lucky 14

Before I Lost You 16

The First Bird 17

Parachutes 18

Petrichor 19

Theft 20

Stickers 21

Skater 23

Morning Sky 24

Paper Doll 25

For my family

VARIOUS DISTANCES

I still can see you,
on the steps without
a coat,

because I said
it wouldn't rain.

The spots on your new shirt
were distant suns
that would outlive us.

SETTING FIRES

The first fire
was a mistake.

It spread
open
like a seed, splintering.

You clutched
your face
with dirt-streaked hands

as the air around you cracked

and split
with heat. Your eyes
went red.

You drew fires

in all your notebooks,
fat and angry: allergies

everyone said,
turning away.

The second one was easier:

a cigarette
dropped out the window.

By the third
you had a plan: an empty
wood

where the sun leaned
like a canvas.

You watched trucks come from the town
with their red lights
like tiny prayers.

You pulled
the smoke into your lungs, holding it tight
like it might

save you.

LOOSE

When the wind lifts
just the ends

of my loose hair, I think
of summer

of my uncles on the porch
smoking Marlboros

and the sky in the black
trees,
disappearing.

From the road, their cigarettes
were distant
cities,

unafraid
of what they'd done. They couldn't
sleep.

In my room with the door shut
I'd pull my shirt
over my head and the dim

light came
through the fabric so it looked
as thin as paper—a ghost

life,
dull and quiet
as a folded photograph.

Cars went past, one

by one, with their headlights on, as bright
as surging

pain.

THE BABY

Her heartbeat
might

have hounded you,
like guilt,

and so you buried her

the way
you hid the baby books you looked at,

stuffing them
down in your bag.

You never brought them
back. Was it stealing?

No one talks about the boy, now,
anyway.

You wore a hole
in his old sweatshirt,
where your thumb

pushed through the sleeve
and then nobody else

would take it.

YELLOW HOUSE

My father stopped the car;
the street was full of ice. We looked
out at the yellow house.

Our breath against the windows
was like fire, eating the house.

It was the house my father lived in,
once, when he was young, dark now
as the inside of a lung.

The sky was pale as ash, and
exhaust behind the car trembled like ghosts.
We were the ghosts, worn thin and soft.
Sun against the ice glinted like eyes.

VELELLA

We found them
on the beach that afternoon,
as blue as bruises.

Like an army, or
a thousand

frightened cows, standing
together

for protection. They had fins

the width
of fingernails, smudged
as warping glass.

I learned later
that what's left is not
the body—that

the dry lace on the beach
by the next day

is meaningless

without the rest, as blank
and joined
as paper dolls.

We stepped

around them finding
flat palms of smooth sand, cool

and familiar, but

that night at the motel I watched
the dull slick of the water
from the window

with my cold breath leaving marks
on the frail pane
while you slept.

By the next morning, they had dried
to narrow chains

wrapped round

each other.

BATS

The bats
lace like shy fingers

overhead, but
this is marriage, after

all. You wake him up.

You pull
the covers to your chin
watching them

fly; you hold

his arm.

The bats are flecks of ash;
you are the fire—

if there was fire—

hot and shaking
in the bed
in the hotel. What

does it mean, if there are bats in a hotel? You
are afraid. Are they trapped? Later on
you read

the bats are getting sick, that
they are dying, and nobody

can say why. There are pictures
of a bat, in a blank cave, with his eyes
shut. Somebody stood there, taking pictures,
while he slept.

Your husband leaves, but
you can only dream

of bats: their faces close
and their mouths open.

When you drive, after that, you look for them

in the thin sky
but never see them.

COYOTES

Coyotes on the hill
across the lake

are scattered stones. Sharp
high barks. You listen

lying flat, awake
in the old tent. (It was your
father's: thin

and gray as a weak
lung.

My escape

he said, packing on a Friday, kneeling hard
on the lean fabric
to force out unwanted

air.) Your breath

catches
on the nylon; makes
it cry.

You wonder if your father lay here
all alone, with the

limp pulse
of the water in his ears like a reminder.

Did he think about coyotes

about children

with their smiles
and vacant eyes

just across town?

DOCKS

We used to drive
to the old movie house
in your dead brother's car

and pay to watch
the midnight horror
shows.

I'd bite my palm
but never hard enough
to bleed.

Sometimes your
hand would reach
for my hand, in the dark,

and it made me think
of boats:

how, after we left,

they'd rest against
the docks

in the dark water.

LUCKY

In the car, you trace
the leather of the seatback
with your hand.

Your hand looks just
like your mother's in the dark.
Your veins are straws. Hard
and hollow

and so thin.

The judge they picked,
with the sad eyes, told you to come to the old prison
to surrender, but you don't know what to think

on the way there. You see the streetlight
on your cheek; you think
of nothing

of your children

of your hair,
in the clean window,
smooth and rich. You put your hand

against the glass, and it is cold.

You are so lucky,
someone said at that one party, normal people
would have gone to jail

for life. Don't
think of that. You think of stars,

above the car, like frightened children,
and you brush

back your smooth hair with shaking fingers. You are

lucky, you say, once,
in the dark car, you are so

lucky.

BEFORE I LOST YOU

It was August—
dumb with heat.

The sweat against my neck
was an old scar—a flash
of gold.

Our thighs burned
on the seat

of the old fishing boat
your father never used.

On the reservoir we drifted over canyons,
kicked our feet swimming a mile above
old riverbeds and skeletons
of trees.

We didn't realize that water was a grave:
bright and stunned.

I still think of your pale hand,
on the boat's thin metal heart,

pressing gently.

THE FIRST BIRD

You find the rain of tiny bodies
in the morning, damp and flecked with newborn
frost. Some

are small enough to rest
inside your palm: starlings,
thrushes. A small owl. A wood-

brown sparrow. You

were raised in an apartment, where the sky
hung on the wall inside the building. When

you saw the first bird hit, you held
your hand against your throat
and said a prayer.

Its wings fell open, smashed in flat
as broken plates. You thought

of planes,
draped in blood, their windshields
cracked. No one came

for the first bird, so
you went down
to the gray street

and lifted it, its limp feet trailing down your wrist.

You told yourself you would make sure
to learn

its name.

PARACHUTES

The moon is low and sharp tonight,
It hangs above the Coast Range like a fingernail,
Poised to scratch the end off of the street.

Behind it I can see its softened heft:
Swollen as an eyeball's dim insides,
Full of holes.

I think about us, driving on 140 toward
The mountains, with our pasts puffed out
Like dirty parachutes that might
Not save us anyway.

PETRICHOR

During the last storm
the rain

made islands on the windshield: clear
and round

as forming questions.

You sat with me
and we traced out soft new maps

with shaking fingers—here
is how

I'd get to you, losing
myself

in the blank water. But
it hasn't rained

in months,
and the dust falls

in soft sheets on your old car. There still
are patterns

on the glass
left there like shadows.

When I drive
I see the rain

pressed to the street, your fingers
flattening the drops
like ironed bedclothes, smoothing them

with one vague hand.

THEFT

The jewelry scattered like a cough:

an aunt wearing her necklace,
and her rings prone on my mother's desk.

The days raised up their arms,
then brought them down.

I took the shamrock charm she'd
worn on a gold bracelet, once, for luck.

Its edges made thin lines against my palm.

I thought of hands and ears and throats
and empty spaces left in rings.

She wouldn't let them take the cross on a gold chain
that she wore to be confirmed.

Now it is as empty as a dented can, left out on the road, but
the charm is in my pocket, dark and hard.

STICKERS

After my cousin killed
himself, I thought

about his bedroom
with the stickers on the walls. Super
heroes,

with their arms as thick as
paper.

One July,
we lay inside on a warm night
and told ghost stories

while our parents
smoked and talked beneath the window. I could hear

our mothers arguing outside, and he said
this house is a haunted place. I
laughed

and didn't ask
about the blank tear on his cheek like a white scar
or his new school.

He said shut up.

Later on, I wondered how long it would be
until his mother scraped

those stickers off the walls
to sell the house. I thought of her

in his bright room
all by herself

doing the best that she could do

and the strongest men on earth
coming apart

beneath her nails.

SKATER

Short blue shorts
and wide pale legs, knees

bent
like broken glasses. Oh
I wish

you
everything:

smooth
flat floors

when you lean
forward,

  your arms open.

MORNING SKY

We couldn't tell when it would happen.

The sky would tap
The windows, pink as fingertips.

An accident of clouds and light, as
Cold as thinning air.

It wasn't anything
That anyone could touch.

When people tell me ways they
Found a god, I always think of clouds—of my bare feet
Flat on the floor

All the windows lit like love.

PAPER DOLL

On the tape
you are so thin—
a paper

doll.

It is raining
(on the tape)

and you are
dancing

with a boy
on tilted
streets, and your hair

is like soft yarn,
stuck to your shoulders.

I can't tell

how old you are.

It is raining
(in our town, outside my window)

and I'm tired, and I'm
watching

these old movies, one by one.
Versions
of you

skate
around me, leaving
lines—long

lean scars—

on everything.

Elizabeth McMunn-Tetangco lives in California's Central Valley with her husband and son. She co-edits *One Sentence Poems,* an online journal of short poetry, and also works as a librarian. In addition to writing and reading, she enjoys running with her dog, kayaking, and exploring as much of the world as she possibly can. Her poems have appeared in a number of different publications, and she is grateful to Finishing Line Press for giving them a home.

www.ingramcontent.com/pod-product-compliance
Lightning Source LLC
LaVergne TN
LVHW041518070426
835507LV00012B/1654